WHOLESALING REAL ESTATE
A Beginners Guide

BRENT D. DRISCOLL

INTRODUCTION

Real estate - owning it is the American Dream. It is a symbol of wealth and status. It has been so for generations and it will be so as long as there is an open market and land to sell.

If you look into the background and history of the wealthiest Americans, 9 times out of 10 you will discover that they used real estate as a stepping stone to wealth.

Investing in real estate gives the everyday person like you or me the opportunity to get into the game. It gives us a chance to build that wealth and status. To create passive income that compounds into freedom.

Real estate IS the great equalizer. In fact, with wholesaling you do not even need to have a bank account packed with tens of thousands of dollars. You can start investing in real estate with very little investment.

Wholesaling real estate is a popular buzz word. Anyone who talks about investing in property; reads books about how to get rich quick or visits real estate investor forums has heard about wholesaling. What is it all about? How does this really work? Is it a scam or is it legit? Can I make money with it?

I am going to take the opportunity to answer all those questions and more. The goal of this book is to not only show you how wholesaling works, but also how you can get into the business. As a guide to wholesaling, this book will teach you the difference between wholesaling properties and flipping real estate.

It will also show you where to look to find the best deals and how to recognize a good deal from a loser. It will also teach you where to find sellers and buyers and how to market to them.

We will instruct you on how to protect yourself and your investments while working in this competitive marketplace. That will include guidelines on working with licensed real estate agents along with how to write an offer that protects you and your end buyer.

When you finish reading this short guide, you will have the confidence and the ability to begin wholesaling and to begin earning money for you and your family.

Wholesaling is not just about the money; however, it is about freedom. It is the freedom to earn limitless income. It is the freedom to work for yourself. It is the freedom to set your own hours. It is the freedom to go to your daughter's dance recital in the middle of the day. It is the freedom to have a life.

Real estate wholesaling is not your traditional way of playing in the property market. It is much more fluid; much more flexible and much more creative. You do not need an office. You do not need a website. You do not even need a real estate license. Once you have learned the basics, you can jump right in and start making deals tomorrow.

Do you want that kind of freedom?

Okay then. Let's not wait any longer! Let's jump in and get started in the exciting, adrenaline pumping, fast acting field of real estate wholesaling.

CHAPTER 1 WHAT IS REAL ESTATE WHOLESALING?

Wholesaling properties is almost as different from traditional real estate investing as day is to night. Traditional real estate investments involve two basic approaches.

Buy and Hold

A buy and hold is just what it seems. You buy a property which is generally going to be used as a rental and then you hold on to it. This investment generates an income stream with the potential for future property appreciation when you sell.

Buy and Flip

Property flipping is the act of purchasing a piece of real estate for less than market value (either through price or because of condition) and then reselling it at a higher price (often after you have fixed up the property).

Wholesaling real estate is a whole different ballgame.
Though at first glance it is similar to a Buy and Flip but there are critical differences.

Buy and Flip deals require the buyer to pay for the property purchase either with cash or through financing.

Wholesale transactions never transfer the title to the wholesaler. The wholesaler only acts as the middleman in the transaction. You do not have to pay for the real estate. You do not have to go get a bank loan because you never own the property.
Wholesaling is simply transferring your contracted interest in the property for a fee.

This is a critical point. You must understand this concept clearly before moving forward.

The goal of a wholesaler, real estate or otherwise, is to obtain a product for cheap and then sell it for more. The difference in price is the wholesaler's profit.

> **Example:**
> Wholesaler buys an auctioned car for $1,500.
> The retail value is $3,500.
> The wholesaler sells the car for retail price.
> The profit off the deal is $2,000.

The same holds true for wholesaling real estate *except* you never actual buy the property. You are selling your right to buy the property. You are selling your purchase contract not the actual real estate. This is why you do not need a real estate license to be a wholesaler.

Wholesaling is selling a contract NOT real estate.

> **Example:**
> Owner needs to sell his house right now.
>   "As Is," the house is worth $50,000.
> Wholesaler offers $35,000 cash.
>   Seller accepts offer.
> Wholesaler calls his client who is looking for houses.
>   He offers to sell the house for $45,000.
>   The end buyer accepts.
> Wholesaler uses the end buyer's money to pay the seller's
>   sales price of $35,000.
>   The title is placed in the end buyer's name.
> Wholesaler keeps $10,000.

Think about this.

> **Did the wholesaler ever own the property?**
>   No, he only "owned" the purchase contract.

Did the wholesaler spend any of his own money?
No, he used his end buyer to finance the deal.

Was anyone scammed or taken advantage of?
No, the seller needed a buyer right away. Sure he could have gotten a full price seller if he had waited, but maybe he would have lost the house to foreclosure by then.

The end buyer was looking for the right house. The wholesaler did him a service and found one for him – and below market value at that.

Both parties got what they wanted AND the wholesaler pockets $10k as the middleman.

Is real estate wholesaling a good place for new real estate investors to get started?

Wholesaling is an excellent way for a new real estate investor to jump right into the property market. You do not need to have much cash to start. You do not need to get approved for bank financing. You do not even need to have good credit. Anyone can start wholesaling once they acquire the skills.
Wholesaling can be used for two end games.

End Game #1
You can keep on wholesaling properties, earning money with each transaction. This income can be used as the equivalent of wages. You could even quite your job and do this full time.

End Game #2
You could use wholesaling as a way to build cash to invest in buy and hold real estate. Or you could use the cash to buy run down properties and rehab them. These properties are then resold for a profit.

Wholesaling can be an end game all on its own or you can use it as a stepping stone into more permanent real estate investing. No matter what your end game, wholesaling is a great way to enter into the property market.

What is the income potential of a real estate wholesaler?

Answering that question is like asking a Realtor how much money you can make selling property. It depends.

It depends on where you are located. Wholesaling properties in the hills of Kentucky is going to earn you substantially less than wholesaling in San Francisco.

It depends on what you wholesale. As you gain experience, you are going to find your niche. Is it abandoned properties? How about tired landlords that are offloading their rentals? Or will you focus on mid-range single family homes?

It depends on the real estate market. The real estate market is never stagnant. It is always changing. Just a few years ago it was a huge buyer's market with dirt cheap prices, but times are changing and with fewer properties for sale, it is quickly favoring the seller. Depending on the market, the spread between the discounted purchase and the resale price will be variable.

For the sake of argument, however, let's just run through a few thoughts here. If we step away and look at the big picture, it might look something like this:

Some deals might mean that you walk away with $200 where as others may earn you $20,000. Each deal will be different.

If you focused on locating properties that are less than

$50,000 and you decided to mark them up by only 5%; then when you put a $50k property under contract, you would make $2,500. What if you closed on only 2 properties a month? Would you like to make $5,000 a month?

Instead, you decide to focus on middle-income homes in the $200 - $300,000 price range because that is where there is the highest demand from buyers. If you only marked these already discounted properties by $10,000, you would only have to close one transaction a month to earn $120,000 a year.

Can you see the endless amount of possible income? Do you earn this kind of wage where you are working right now? Does it look like more income and less hours? Perhaps. But there is a catch...

Real estate wholesaling **is not easy money**. This false thinking is fed to gullible entrepreneurs who are looking for quick cash and minimal effort by "wholesaling gurus" just wanting to make money off their programs.

Wholesaling means a lot of footwork. There is a lot time and focus involved in this field. It requires endurance, dedication and commitment. You will need to be self-driven and motivated. Having excellent people skills and superb negotiating abilities are also important qualities to possess.

Thinking that you are going to get rich quick is only a recipe to failure. Think of wholesaling as a business. Look at it as a job replacement (and the word "job" is synonymous with effort right?). It will require learning a skill set and having some startup cash.

How much money do I need to start?
If we are going to look at real estate wholesaling as a business,

then your startup costs will depend on how big of a business that you want all at once.

There are ways to start this business with only a cell phone, an internet connection and a scrap of paper.

But more often than not, someone just starting in wholesaling will need to build a network and get the word out relatively quickly in order to get some deals moving. Usually this requires obtaining mailing lists (either by hand or through purchase), creating marketing materials (letters or postcards) and paying for postage. There is also the cost to create bandit signs (which we will explain later) and setup some type of phone system to handle the response to your mailings.

Wholesaling is more about marketing than about real estate. You do not need money to buy a property but you will need money to market the property.

You're looking for a number here right? I really hate to give you one since the more you spend on marketing, the more response you will get. The more response you get, the more properties you can get under contract. The more properties under contract, the more deals you can close.

But, I will tell you this, you do not need $5,000 to start. Dig up at least $500 and you can get your foot in the door.

CHAPTER 2 FIND YOUR TARGET AREA

It is a fact of life that you cannot do everything at once. Ever hear of the "Jack-of-all-trades master of none"? That is *not* what we want in real estate.

If you want to play a role in the game, then you have to pick a side and play your position. The goalie cannot decide one day that he wants to play defense. He needs to take his position and master it.

The same is true in real estate. You need to choose your market area and master it. Becoming an expert in your specific area will not only make it easier to identify great deals but it will also build credibility and trust – two essential qualities when it comes to performing well in the real estate market.

Become an expert in that specific area.

Wholesaling property is a matter of being able to find a property whereby you can get it under contract for less than the market value and then turn around and sell that contract for at or near market value. But how can you find these properties? What makes a good deal? What are buyers looking for? Who are the buyers? Where is the market going?

The answers to these questions come from understanding the length, width and depth of your particular market area. You need to spend the time to become an expert in your field – an expert in finding, negotiating and marketing real estate deals.

Before you begin, you first need to choose your market area.

Become clear on your target.

Before you start wholesaling, you are going to need to **pick a**

market to perform in. While there may be more active markets or even more profitable ones, the market area where you live is going to be the easiest one to master.

Whether you recognize it or not, you already know the underlying flavor of your area. You know who lives there; who would move into the area; the style of homes; what areas are "on the other side of the tracts" and even where future growth may happen. Just living and interacting in your town, suburb or city has taught you much.

What you know, however, is not enough. It only makes you a native but not an expert.
You need to look at your market area through the eyes of an investor and not as a homeowner.

The next time you drive through your market area, focus on looking at the homes you are passing. Do you see homes that are abandoned? Run down? In desperate need of renovation? What neighborhoods are being rejuvenated? What neighborhoods are turning into slums? Where are the areas that have growth potential – either through expansion, rejuvenation or transition? How many bank owned properties are in any given neighborhood? Are these still impacting your market area?

Now, change your focus. Look at your market area through the eyes of an end buyer. What types of homes have all the "For Sale" signs in the yard? How quickly are they selling? Who are buying these homes? Are they first home buyers, retirees, couples, families, move-ins, investors or landlords? What are buyers looking for in a home? What types of home features are in demand? Do you see a shift in buying (i.e. from large estates to smaller homes; houses to condominium developments; single family homes to rental properties.)

From this analysis you should have a better grasp of what is going on in your market area. Now is the time to get a second opinion. Your best source of information is going to be from experienced real estate agents. Every market has some top performers. They are the faces that you see on all the yard signs. These people know their market and they have the data to back it up. This can be a great start to building your network.

You want their data. Here is how you get it.
Before we jump into that deep side of the pool, I want to take a moment to explain how to work with real estate agents. Realtors have a general distrust and genuine dislike of wholesalers. Many of them view us as people who have pushed into their field without a license and are there to steal business away from them.

How you approach a Realtor will determine if you further that perception or change it.
At some point as a wholesaler, you are going to need some real estate agents playing on your team. They have a role to play just like you have. You need to assure them that you both are not playing (or fighting for) the same position.

You are always going to approach real estate agents as an investor. *Do not tell them you are a wholesaler.* You are an investor. What you do with your investment 30 seconds after owning it is your business – not theirs.

When you contact this top performing real estate agent, be straight up with them. Do not act like you are hiding something (because you're not). Do not treat them like you are prying information out of them and plan to give them nothing in return (because you're not). This is the first step to measuring the potential of bring this agent into your team. Treat them with respect and acknowledge their experience and professionalism.

Perhaps you could say something like this:

> *"Joe Reator, I am really glad you could take a few minutes to meet with me today. I am seriously looking to get into property investments. I haven't decided whether I should*

get into the rental market or look into fixer-uppers. What is your take of the market? What would you recommend?"

Now, sit back and listen. You could even take some notes if you like (which shows your serious and may get them to talk more). If they rattle off a list of sales statistics, ask if you could get a printout to take home and review. You could further the discussion by asking:

"So Joe, if you were going to start investing, what types of properties would have the best potential for a return and why?"

"What type of person is your typical buyer, an investor or a homeowner? What kinds of properties are your investors looking for? How about homeowners; what do they want?"

"Do you think we are still being affected by the foreclosure crisis? What would you say is the percentage of your active listings that are distressed properties? Are they affecting the market value of other properties?"

At this point, you have created a nice give and take relationship. You have gotten a first impression of him or her and they have gotten a first impression of you. Now it is time to get a little bit more quantitative data from them.

"Joe, could I ask a favor? Before I seriously start looking for some properties, would you be willing to give me some market statistics? I would be interested in getting some information that would include the average percentage of change between listing and sales prices and the average day on the market. Does your MLS software prepare reports like that? If so, could I please get a copy? Are there any other statistics that could help me?"

This meeting should have either validated your personal research or pointed you in a direction that you may not have considered.

Now it is time to start analyzing the hard data. It is time to look at the comps.

How to get comps.

Getting reliable data for this stretch of the game is critical. It cannot be overstressed. If your market study data is off, then all your offers will be off. You need to get some trustworthy data.

There is a plethora of data on the internet but just because it's free does not mean it's true.

Many inexperienced wholesalers and investors rely on Trulia and Zillow to "run their comps." This is one of the biggest mistakes you could make in your business. Let me explain why.

Redfin recently conducted a study of the reliability of Trulia and Zillow. Their report stated that these two sites are missing around 20% of the active listings and that it takes 7 to 9 days before a new listing is uploaded. Additionally, 36.5% of their active listings are no longer for sale.

What does this actually mean? In active markets, not seeing a listing for 9 days could very well mean that great deal is already gone. What you are looking at are the mid-to-high priced homes that have no wholesale potential. On top of that, 35% of your time is wasted because you are researching listings that no longer exist. And if that wasn't bad enough, for every 80 homes you considered, you missed seeing 20 possibilities. Does that sound like a good business practice?

How about estimating property value? Zillow can provide you with a free estimate. But how accurate is their estimate? According to Zillow's own Zestimate data accuracy report, they have a median error rate of 6.9%. In fact, further down in their report they state that only 38.3% of the time are they within 5%

of the actual sales price. The reality is that they are 20% off the actual sales price 84.7% of the time.

In the wholesaling business, a 20% mistake in pricing is suicidal. Follow the Zestimate's price recommendations and you could very well lose all your profit on every deal.

Where can I find good comps?

Finding good comps does not mean that you have to pester your new real estate agent friend day and night. Nope. There are reliable sources of listed properties on the internet. Try these on for size:

- Redfin
- Realtor.com
- Local Brokerage Websites

Local brokerage websites are going to have the most up-to-date information. Just do a search for local real estate businesses and then bookmark them for future reference.

When you find a sold property, you can either call the listing agent or your realtor friend and kindly ask for the sales price. You may need to explain that you are doing an investor's market study and will be using the information to help make more realistic offers.

What to do with the data.

Now that you have access to lots and lots of raw data, it is time to convert that data to something that you can use. This data is going to be used on both sides of the playing field. It is going to help you analyze properties to see if you should make an offer. It will also help you know the true market value for an end buyer.

To assemble your data, you should make a spreadsheet. Along the top row create the following column headers:

- Address
- List Price
- Lot Size
- Home Sq. Ft.
- List Price/SF
- BR/BA
- List Price/BR
- Basement/Finished
- Garage/# Cars
- Amenities
- Sales Price
- Sales Price/SF
- Sales Price/BR
- % Diff. LP:SP
- DOM

Each property will be put into one row. You can even assign a hyperlink to the property address as a reference.

You want to break the list price down to the price per square foot (List Price/SF) and the price per bedroom (List Price/BR). At the bottom of your spreadsheet, setup a row labeled "MEDIAN TOTALS." Then under each breakdown column insert a formula to compute the median price. To keep apples to apples, you may want to create a spreadsheet for each category of home such as 2 bedroom, 3 bedroom and 4 + bedroom for starters.

The purpose of this spreadsheet is to break the list price (and hopefully the sales price) down to comparable numbers that you can apply to other properties. After compiling, say 50 listings, you will be able to figure out what is the average price per square foot and how to compute the property value off the number of bedrooms.

For example:

Let's say that the median list price for a 2 bedroom/1

bath home is $72.00 per square foot and the price per bedroom is $32,000.

If you find a 900 square foot house with 2 BR/1BA, the list price based on the size should be $64,800. Based on the number of bedrooms it should be $64,000.

If your records show that these types of properties have a list price discounting of 5%. Then the most likely sales price would be $61,180 or rounded to $61,200. *(Formula: [average $64,800 and $64,000 = $64,400] x .95)*

If the property is listed for $72,900 then you have to ask yourself why. Was it renovated? Does it have extra land? Is there a basement? Is it finished? Is there a garage? Is it any different than the average property in this price group? If not, then walk away.

But, what if the property is listed for $51,500 and it is similar to most of the properties in your spreadsheet. Now you need to look a little further. This property may be a candidate to consider.

Of course, this is a very very broad analysis. As you gain experience, you may want to add columns for quality, construction style, neighborhood, etc. This will help you to better match the property under consideration with your database of comps.

This first phase of becoming a property wholesaler may seem tedious, but without it you are just a blind soccer player. Your time is worth money. An investment of time now will save you money in the future – guaranteed. In fact, it *will* make you money and it will make you money very soon.

CHAPTER 3 HOW TO FIND YOUR FIRST SELLER

This is where the business begins. Without sellers and their properties, you cannot do business. You will find that this part of your wholesaling business is where you will spend a lot of your time – but it is time and money well spent.

Many new wholesalers find it difficult to locate properties to wholesale. They start by looking at properties that are in the Multiple Listing Service or MLS and then they wonder why they cannot find any good deals.

Why You Shouldn't Rely on the MLS.

Though on the surface, this looks like a nice easy place to find cheap properties; the problem here is that you will rarely find a highly discounted property. In order to earn money, you must be able to "resell" these properties for more than what you offered to pay.

The real estate market, as handled by licensed real estate agents, is not geared toward liquidating properties. Realtors work on commission. Though they want to quickly sell a property, they also do not want to throw away income. This means that they will encourage buyers to market their homes at or near market value.

Yes, there are discounted homes here. But look twice. These homes usually have some sort of stigma – drug house, trashed by the tenant, bad foundation, empty foreclosure etc. If it is a non-stigmatized home, then the discounting you will find is not generally going to be over 10 – 15%. This is going to severely affect your profit margin.

I am not saying that you should write off the MLS, but do not solely rely on it. Plus, when you find a great deal, remember that you will be competing with every other buyer, Realtor and investor that has access to that same listing.

There are better places, however, to look for cheaper property deals.

Using Craigslist

Craigslist is a great source of information and leads. New listings of properties in your market area arrive here daily. Though many of these will be MLS listed properties, you will find tons of "For Sale by Owner" (FSBO) properties. These are great leads!

Also, do not overlook the properties that are listed for rent. Perhaps you will find a burnt-out and exhausted landlord that would just love to dump his properties (and his management headache) in exchange for some immediate cash.

Craigslist can also be used on the proactive side as well. You can post ads that are similar to bandit sign advertisements.

Bandit Signs

Here is another up-and-coming buzz word that you must be hearing a lot. Bandit signs are a guerilla marketing technique where you put signs anywhere and everywhere that is legally possible.

Have you ever seen these signs on street corners and in yards? Those are bandit signs and they are super effective.

You can get them made locally or through ordering them online. Put on them a number that is only dedicated to incoming calls. You can also add a website address if you have setup one.

Mailing Lists

This is perhaps the most expensive marketing option while pursuing seller leads, but it is also the option that pays off multiple times over what you spend.

Mailing lists are effective because they reach potential sellers that may not even be thinking of selling their home. Or perhaps they just got a Notice of Default threatening foreclosure on the same day you sent them a postcard offering to buy their home.

When you send a letter or a postcard, these can be kept for later unlike bandit signs that can be removed or forgotten or a Craigslist ad that gets lost in the shuffle. Some sellers have hung onto my postcards for months, only to give me a call when they are ready.

There are two ways to create a mailing list:

Use your leads.
No matter who they are, if you get any type of call back off your advertising materials, it is a lead. Even if the caller hung up or wasn't interested in selling – it is still a lead. Who knows what will happen in their life tomorrow to change their mind. Every single lead needs to be recorded in a mailing list.

You have their phone number; now just use the internet to get their mailing address through a reverse directory search.

Purchased Specific Lists

Another source of possible sellers is the purchased mailing list. These lists are highly targeted and can be focus to the types of sellers you are looking for. These lists can be a great way to jump into wholesaling without spending gobs and gobs of time hunting for leads.

Check out these websites that I use:

> ListSource
> USLeadList

When it comes to mailing lists, the more specific the list the greater your response rate will be. Expect to get a 1- 2% response rate with a bulk mailing to general zip codes. If you target that list to specific groups, then you could receive a response rate of 15% (which is really good).

Target demographics that respond well to mailings and have an above average response rate include:

Absentee Sellers
This represents the group of property owners that are out-of-state. They do not have a direct involvement with the property and thus may be more than willing to let it go.

Divorcees
After going through a nasty divorce, many soon to be ex-couples will need to sell their home and divide the profits. Often the faster this can happen, the happier they will be. In walks the wholesaler.

Foreclosure Victims
During this tragic and highly stressful time, a majority of homeowners will be unable to stop a bank foreclosure – either they are too behind in the payments or they have waited too long before acting. You can come in as the hero and help them out.

Estate Inheritance Heirs

Reading a will can be an exciting time (though sad) for family members – that is unless Uncle Rufus has left his favorite city-loving nephew his 1950's hunting cabin. The wholesaler steps in offering to exchange cold hard cash for his unwanted property.

The more targeted your mailing list; the better will be your response rate. Once you have established a good list, you should regularly be mailing marketing materials (yellow letters or postcards) to them.

Speaking of marketing materials, you are going to need that too. The most common are:

Yellow Letters

Yellow letters basically refers to a letter that is hand written and very informal, as you can see in the picture here. The envelopes are handwritten and it is sent with a first class stamp.

These letters are usually opened because they do not look like standard bulk advertising material.

With a little skill, these can be computer generated. Just remember, however, that it is easy to identify the computer's "handwritten" font. You can, however, scan a sample letter in your computer and just leave blanks for the areas you need to fill in by hand.

Dear (owner's name)

Hi!

My name is John Williams and I would like to

$ BUY $

your house at (property address)

Please call me at
#

Thanks!
John

Just make sure that the computer ink and your pen color are identical in thickness and color.

If you would like to send something a little more professional, I have found the following letter format quite effective:

> *Dear (Owner's Name):*
>
> *I was driving around in your area and noticed your house and was wondering if you might be interested in discussing selling it or another property you might own. One of the areas I work in is buying houses that need some repair and rehabbing the property to improve its appearance and value.*
>
> *I am local real estate investor that buys properties in (name your area) area. I am able to buy properties quickly for cash and usually can close within 30 days or less.*
>
> *The typical process is a preliminary discussion over the phone to obtain some basic information. If that conversation is mutually agreeable then we can arrange for me to come by and take a look at your home to get a better understanding of its condition and what repairs may be needed. Then, we can work toward a fair selling price for your home.*
>
> *If you are interested, you can either provide me with a phone number where you can be reached or if you prefer you can call me at (your phone number) or via email at (your email address)*
>
> *Sincerely,*
>
> *(Your Name)*

Because of their size, however there will be more mailing expense compared to postcards. The cost to mail a first-class envelope is currently $0.70. That is in addition to the cost of the paper, ink and envelope.

Postcards
Postcards are another very effective marketing tool to locate sellers. These work well for mass mailings where you are unsure if all on this mailing list are going to be motivated to sell.

Perhaps the strongest appeal to postcards is their cost. They are cheaper to produce, do not require envelopes and are cheaper to mail. The current rate to mail a postcard is $0.34 for a 6" x 4 ¼" postcard.

There are plenty of companies online and off that can produce, and even mail, your postcards for you. I would recommend these:
> Click2Mail
> VistaPrint

Though postcards are smaller and cheaper, they require more effort to make sure they grab the reader's attention. There are some essential elements to designing a postcard.

- A clear headline.
- An appropriate graphic.
- Eye catching color choices.
- Intriguing statement on the back to keep them reading.
- A list of the benefits of calling you.
- Enticing offer.
- Your company name and logo.
- Call to action
- Contact information.

The Call to Action
The call to action is perhaps the most critical part of an advertisement – other than your contact information, of course.

Unless you can motivate your reader to action, your marketing has failed.

You are not just getting the word out that you exist. You want them to contact you. An effective call to action can increase your conversion rate dramatically. This is an item that definitely requires thought, tweaking and second opinions. A small change here can make all the difference in the world.

Here is some advice from marketing experts:

- **Use actionable language.**
  Instead of "Be Smart" say something like "Discover," "Unearth" or "Find."
- **Include a clear value proposition.**
  You need to clearly state why they should call you whether you are offering "Quick Cash," or "Help to Stop Foreclosures" or "If you need to sell your home today call..."
- **Play up Time-Sensitivity.**
  Move them to call today, not to put the postcard on a "To-Do" stack. Show them time is of the essence. This could be with a statement like "Call now while funds are available!" or "Do not wait, call today."
- **Use Contrasting Colors.**
  Your call to action needs to stand out. Contrasting colors help to make sure this doesn't blend in with the rest of your postcard.
- **Make it Big.**
  If you want them to call you, then make your phone number stand out. If you want them to go to your website, make sure your website address is easy to remember.
- **Test Several Options**
  What you think may work and what actually gets a response could be vastly different. Try testing a couple of different calls to action by using one mailing list but splitting it between two different postcards. Then

carefully monitor who got what and who responds. This will help you develop a bang-on marketing campaign.

By-the-way, this is *not* a one-time mailing. Why are TV commercials so effective? Advertisers know that you will not run out and by their stuff off the first advertisement. But they do know that if you see their ad over and over and over, it will build a desire for item no matter how ridiculous. (I mean someone has to be getting rich off the can of spray hair paint for balding males. Someone is buying it.)

The same will hold true with your mailings. Yes, they are probably going to throw the first postcard in the trash. But how about the second, the third, the 10th. Over time they will no doubt give you a call – just like the guy that buys the can of hair paint that he never thought he wanted.

Tracking Your Response Rate

You could spend thousands on different forms of marketing, but if you do not create a system for measuring the success of your marketing, then you will never know which marketing tool is not working at all and which is generating a higher return on the money you have spent.

This entails measuring the dollars you are spending on each campaign versus the percentage of response.

> For example, if you spend $100 on bandit signs and get 8 leads within 30 days. It will have cost you $12.50 to get that lead. If one of those 8 leads signs a contract, then that contract cost you $100.

> On the other hand, if you spent $2,500 on mailing a total of 3,000 yellow letters and postcards and had a call back rate of 4.5%, you would have created 135 leads. Each lead cost you $18.51. If of those 135 leads, you closed 5 deals, then each contract cost you $500.

At this point, you can see that your bandit signs are generating a more profitable response. Do not give up on your mailings, however, but make sure you are maximizing your bandit sign marketing and perhaps creating a better targeted mailing.

An expense of $500 per contract seems like a lot of money doesn't it? But that contract will on the average yield between $3,000 and $7,000. Are you willing to spend $500 to make $7,000 on one deal? Are you willing to shell out $2,500 in marketing to make $6,000? In my opinion, that is a great return on your investment. Try finding a stock or mutual fund that will give you that return.

> But what if you tweaked your call to action on your next mailing? What if after spending another $2,500, your response rate jumps to 7%?

> Now you are looking at 210 leads from 3,000 letters. If you can seal 10 contracts, you have reduced your contract expense to $250 each.

Do you see how an effective call to action plus monitoring exactly where your leads are coming from can help you see where to funnel your advertising budget? Spending money on effective advertising will earn you 2 or 3 times more down the road.

To do this, you need to track or measure your callbacks. There are several ways to do this.

Different Advertising: Different Phone Number

One of the most effective ways to measure the response of your marketing is to use a different phone number for each marketing tool. This means that your bandit signs would have one number, your Craigslist ads another and your postcards another. That way, when you get a call back on a number, you know exactly where it came from.

Having multiple numbers is not really that expensive. We have internet services that are perfect for that. There are well known companies like Skype and Google Voice. There are other companies that not only offer phone numbers but answering services as well. A few that are highly recommended are Vumber and CallRail.

Ask Your Lead

Another effective way of measuring your marketing is to simply ask your lead how he or she heard about you. You may want to preference your question by saying that you are doing multiple types of marking and you simply would like to know which one touched them.

Now, don't just ask them, make sure that you have some sort of system to keep track of their response. This could be the simple, but less effective, method of using a pad of paper. However, instead I would recommend getting some sort of CRM (Customer Relationship Management) software. You need to keep track of your mailing lists, leads, your response to those leads and the next action.

There are a lot of different CRM systems out there. Some, such as Realeflow, Freedomsoft, and REI BlackBook are designed for the real estate market. Podio on the other hand is a CRM system that is extremely customizable. It can not only handle all of your clients and lead lists but also track your voicemails and email campaigns. It even works on mobile devices.

Regardless of the lead management system you decide to use – make sure you have a system and that you use it. Make sure that you quickly follow up on *all* leads. Do not let a single lead get lost, forgotten or abandoned. **Leads are the lifeblood of the wholesaler's business.**

The Voicemail System

The more marketing you will do, the greater the number of phone calls you will receive. To care for all those calls, there are several options that you have to choose from:

- **You can answer them all yourself.**
  For those that like to stay in ultimate control, this is the best option. This is also a good choice for those getting into the profession. It gives you immediate contact with the potential client and you can quickly gauge their interest.
- **You can hire an assistant.**
  Who doesn't like walking into your office and having a secretary hand you your messages? It is even nicer if she has fielded all the cranky, irritated and simply curious callers for you. But this method, though helpful and pampered, costs wages. If your business is growing leaps and bounds, this may be a wise option.
- **Get a Voicemail System**
  Here you have the best of both worlds. You get to stay in control but, you can field your calls. (There is a level of satisfaction to hitting "Delete" when you get a message from an irate caller.)

The automated message system is, in my opinion, an absolutely necessary part of the wholesaler's business. Now, I am not talking about the message: "Hi, this is Jeff. I'm not available to take your call right now so please leave a message...BEEEEEEEEP."

No, we are way beyond that. Think of your voicemail system as a "Help Line" or "24 Hotline" (which can be used in your marketing material by the way). You are there to help them. Your business is there to provide a service. (Keep this in mind when talking to your leads – it really helps.)

Have your voicemail educate them for 2 or 3 minutes. If they are calling the mailing list number, explain why you sent them that letter or postcard and how your services can help them. Then ask for a detailed description of the property they are interested in selling and the best way to get a hold of them in the very near future. (Make sure your voicemail will not cut them off.) Thank them for the call and promise to call them back within 24 hours. (Now make sure you keep that promise.)

If you have a website up and running, feel free to include the address in case they would like more information. If you have some sort of draw or promotion, mention it as well. This could be a newsletter ebook or even resources to help fight foreclosure etc.

Sure, you will get more hang-ups with this route – but they probably would have hung up on you if you picked up the phone anyway. Even a hang-up is never lost – thank you Caller ID.

Even a hang-up is a lead. *Always* call them back. If they are not interested in selling now, you still have a lead. It may be a future lead, but it is a lead. Put them on your once-a-month mailing list and see what happens.

Finding and managing your seller leads is a critical part of wholesaling. Take the time to learn how to do this well. Create reasonable systems for keeping track and measuring your incoming leads. And follow up on every lead no matter how small.

Plus, remember where this is all leading to. The $2,500 you spend on effective marketing should generate $6,000 of income. That is your target. That is your goal.

> Vision without action
> is a daydream.
> Action without vision
> is a nightmare.
> ~Japanese Proverb

CHAPTER 4 EVALUATING THE PROPERTY

So you have found a seller that has a property that he or she is willing to sell. Now is the time to learn how to evaluate the property so you can submit a reasonable offer that the seller will hopefully accept *and* one that will also make you money when you sell it to your end buyer.

Here are a few pointers while inspecting the property.

Take pictures inside and out to use in marketing.
While you inspect the property, snap some pictures inside and out. You will use these pictures in your marketing to the end buyer. You can also take pictures of problem areas.

Make sure the pictures are well lit, in focus and identify the layout as well as the positive and negative features of the home.

Look for killer problems.
Though many, if not most, homes that you will be wholesaling will need repairs, remodeling or a complete renovation; there are some properties that should be disregarded. Be very wary of properties that have serious mold or termite problems; those with obvious structural defects; meth houses or tear downs.

How do you determine a purchase price?
This depends on the type of property that you are examining. You will be looking at two basic types of properties – those that need repairs and those that do not. First, you need to know how to figure out the actual market value of a property.

How to Determine the True Market Value
Knowing what a property is *really* worth is extremely important in figuring out how much to offer. Just because it is listed at a

certain price, does not mean that it is worth it. Just because it sold 12 months ago for a certain price does not mean that it is still worth that much.

If you are 10% over on the value of the property, then you will offer too much but your educated end buyer will not pay that much and your profits will take a hit.

Knowing the market value of a property takes experience and time along with resources. Perhaps the easiest way to identify the market value is to analyze comparable sales. These are sales, not listings. What a property is listed for is often not even close to what it sells for. During this stage of the game, you need to use sold data.

How to Find Sold Data?

Remember **your database** of listings and solds? This should help you to figure out the market value either on a per square foot basis or by the number of bedrooms. Remember to add or subtract value for unusual features that are either present or lacking in the property under consideration.

Another source is the **MLS**. There are online sites that offer sold data such as Trulia and Zillow or more accurately Realtor.com and ZipRealty.com. I would highly recommend going onto your local Register of Deeds, whether in person or online, and verifying the sold price and sales date. Accuracy cannot be overstated here.

How about calling your **Realtor friend**? Depending on how well you have developed a working relationship, he or she may be willing to provide some sales information within a price range and a specific area. This is tough ground however. You want to word your request in a way that does not make them think that you are going behind their back and snatching properties. Plan what you are going to say *before* you step foot in their office or pick up your phone.

This seems like a good spot as any to explain the merits of getting your real estate license. Though there is the cost for the education, cost for the license, costs for MLS membership and the requirement to place the license under a Broker; having a real estate license opens up your investment opportunities immensely. You can get direct access to the MLS. You can earn commissions on top of your profit margin. And if you want to get into buy and hold properties, you can earn commissions on your own purchase. What is not to love about that? Plus you will not get nearly the same amount of grief from real estate agents as a wholesaler.

How Much is the "End Buyer's Profit"?

Never forget that you will in the end be "reselling" this property to an end buyer. More often than not, your end buyer is going to be another investor – either a buy and hold or a fix and flip. Either way, they hate (let me say that again "they hate") to pay full price for their investments.

That being said, if you want to keep your investors/end buyers working with you rather than another wholesaler, you need to negotiate deals that give them a sizable slice of the pie as well.

Each buyer is going to be searching for a different discount amount. They are going to tell you some high number (because we all want everything to be on sale all the time) but you need to figure out what they will really work with. Typically you will be looking at a 25 – 35% range. This may come from honest and open conversation or it may come with watching how they respond to the properties that you are presenting to them.

How Much Can I Make on a Deal?

Once you know the true market value of a property and then adjust it for your typical end buyer discount, you now need to remove your profit margin. I personally try to make 10 - 15% off a deal. Depending on your market area and the competition, this could be higher or lower than this number. As you gain experience, you will find a figure that works.

Also, when it comes to your profit margin, it is okay to start small (like 5% or shoot for $500 per deal). Think of it as a way to get into the game and gain valuable firsthand experience. You can always increase your profits as you gain skill as a wholesaler. If you close 4 deals at $500 versus one deal for $2,000, you have earned the same amount of money; probably done the same amount of work but have gained 4 times the experience.

Calculating your maximum purchase price by using a higher profit number at the start will give you, if necessary, a little more leeway to negotiate a more discounted price with your end buyer. When you get down to the last few days before your offer expires, you can lower your profit to sweeten the deal to your buyer and walk away with something rather than nothing.

What to Offer When a Property is in Good Shape

These are the properties that are in relatively good condition. They may not be perfect, but a buyer could generally deal with these minor items on their own. These homes would be move-in ready.

The goal in submitting an offer on a ready home is to accurately determine the true market value and/or your end buyer's price and then subtract your fee. This will reveal what price you should use to submit an offer.

Formula:

Market Value
x .70 End Buyer's Profit
Maximum Sales Price to Your Buyer
x .90 Wholesaler's Profit
Maximum Purchase Price

What to Offer When a Property Needs Repairs

Most of the properties that have the greatest discount potential will be in this category. These homes are in desperate need of repairs, remodeling or complete rehabilitation.

You may find a house that has shag carpet and avocado kitchen appliances with one of those 1970's Formica counters or instead you locate a property that has been gutted by a fire or flooded by a broken pipe. What do you do now?

Determine the repairs and their costs.

Even though you have no intention to buy the house personally, you need to have a general idea of what it will take to fix up the property to get the highest and best price possible. This is what your end buyer will be thinking about. If you want to offer an irresistible deal to your end buyer, then you need to think like your end buyer.

Unless you have a background as a general contractor or experience as a real estate appraiser, you are going to need a second opinion. This is another opportunity to build your team of professionals.

Find a licensed and highly recommended contractor that specializes in rehabilitating or remodeling homes. You will want to bring him to the property and have him take a look around and tell you what he thinks needs to be done to bring the property up to snuff. You will also need a general idea of the costs. (Make sure you bring some paper to take notes.)

Buy the guy lunch, explain what you do and ask for his advice on this property. Explain that you are researching some basic renovation costs for one of your buyers. If he can help you out and provide you with some marketing materials, you will steer your buyers in his direction.

The goal here is to have one or two contractors that you can use to evaluate your properties and give you an idea of the cost of the repairs. Do not waste his time on dud deals or ask for a written report (unless he offers, of course) but pick his brain during the inspection and write everything down. As you gain experience, you will be able to identify repairs and costs on your own.

Remember to keep the repairs realistic and practical. Do not skimp, but do not feel that you have to "fix" everything. Your buyer is only going to spend just enough to get the most return from their investment. Then to be on the safe side and account for the possibility of an error, tack on an additional 10%.

What can increase the value of a property?
There are a few cash cow items when it comes to renovation and remodeling. Not only do these projects have a high rate of return on the investment but they are also in high demand by homeowners.

Small updating projects that have a good return include:

- Entry door replacement
- Garage door replacement.
- Updating fixtures and faucets.
- Replacing trim and molding.
- Replacing door handles and hardware.
- New Paint

Moderate improvement projects that offer a big visual bang for your buck consist of:

- Deck addition (wood).
- New floor coverings.
- Refinishing kitchen cabinets.
- Bathroom remodeling.
- New kitchen appliances.
- New exterior siding.
- Replacing windows.

Large renovation projects need to be weighed carefully as they have the largest cost and easily can go over budget:

- Basement remodel.
- Master bedroom addition.
- New kitchen.
- Attic bedroom.
- Garage addition.

What is the After Repair Value (ARV)?

Now that you have an idea of the cost of the repairs to make this home more appealing and resalable, now is the time to figure out what it will be worth when the repairs are complete.

A big mistake in calculating the ARV is simply adding the total cost of the repairs to the list price. Often renovation costs do not equal resale costs. In the 2014 Cost vs. Value Report produced by Remodeling Magazine, the average return on a remodeling project is only 66.1%. Now this does not account for the rehabber doing the work themselves, but it helps us to understand that you cannot just add the cost of the improvements onto the purchase price.

Talking to your contractors and your real estate agent contacts can be a good source of information. They will have a good idea of the price difference for a home with a remodeled kitchen vs. an old one. They will know how new flooring will affect the value. Remember to keep your notes handy when considering other jobs.

Another way to determine the ARV (after repair value) is to find currently listed homes that represent the remodeled/renovated home. Remember to break them down to the price per unit (square feet or bedrooms) to make sure you are comparing apples to apples.

Never guess on the "After Repair Value." A wrong number here will stalk you through the whole deal. You will have trouble negotiating a contract with the seller and you will find it very difficult to convince a seller *or* you will walk away without a dollar in your hand.

Use this formula.

So you have all the pieces, now it is time to put them all together to calculate the Maximum Purchase Price (MPP). First you need to figure out what the property is worth to your end buyer.

Formula:

> **After Repair Value (ARV)**
> x .70 End Buyer's Profit

<u>- Cost of Repairs</u>
Maximum Sales Price to Your Buyer
<u>x .90 Wholesaler's Profit</u>
Maximum Purchase Price

Let's see how this formula works:

Example:

Seller's List Price	$100,000

After inspecting the property with your contractor...

Estimated Repairs	$17,000

After analyzing other similarly remodeled sold properties...

After Repair Value (ARV)	$132,000

Determine the sales price to your end buyer...

ARV	$132,000
Buyer's Profit Margin	x .70
Subtotal	$92,400
Less Cost of Repairs	- $17,000
Max. Sales Price to Buyer	**$ 75,400**
Wholesaler's Profit Margin	x .95
Maximum Purchase Price	**$71,600**
Less End Buyer's Closing Costs	$4,000
Less Wholesaler's Carrying Costs	$2,000
Target Purchase Price	**$65,600**

I try to include the closing costs as part of the discounting process, but most end buyers will be prepared to cover the costs of closing. This will give you more room to negotiate a higher price with the seller.

I also usually begin by offering 85% of my maximum purchase price ($71,600 x .85 = $60,900, in this example). As long as you can acquire the property for no more than your MPP of $71,600, you will make money. Offering at or below your target purchase price, however, gives you more room to negotiate and the potential for a larger profit margin.

Never be embarrassed of any offer you make. The seller will either accept it, decline it or counter offer. You will never hit a home run unless you swing the bat.

CHAPTER 5 MAKING THE OFFER

We have now reached a critical phase in our wholesaling operation. Up to this point you have studied your market, located some potential sellers and analyzed the physical and financial nature of some possible properties. Now it is time to submit your offer.

Overcoming the Fear of Rejection

Wholesalers must be able to buy their inventory below market value in order to make a profit. Retail sellers want to sell at or above market value to make the largest profit. You are buying from a retail seller, so it can be a challenge to get a below market price.

The key to convincing a retail seller to accept your price requires two factors.

First, the seller must be desperate.
You must find a seller who is highly motivated. They need to sell the property *immediately*. They do not have the time to wait to get a full price offer.

Second, you are there to help them.
You are not in the business of "stealing" or cheating someone out of their homestead. Nope. You are providing a valuable service to help property owners get out of a financial or emotional bind. You are there to *help* them. Never forget that.

Oh yes, you are there to make money. A surgeon works got into the healthcare business to make money, but is he thinking of the new boat he will buy while he is doing open heart surgery? No way, he is focused on helping his patient and he is focused on doing the best job he can.

While wholesaling, if you focus on helping people then you can overcome the fear of rejection. When you are working with the seller, *do not focus on the money.* Focus on help them.

This focus will change your body language, your demeanor and your choice of words. These will soften your low ball offer and ease the shock they will undoubtedly feel after looking at your purchase price.

Identifying the Seller's Needs

If you want to help your seller, then you must identify the reason they are selling. What is their need? If you can satisfy their need, then you will have a greater chance of having them accept your offer.

Why do they want or need to sell their property?

When you originally contacted your seller, you should have learned the answer to this question. Knowing that answer *before* you submit your offer will help you to present your offer in the best possible light.

Foreclosure

If they need to sell because they are facing foreclosure, then unless you want to deal with a short sale (and you don't), then your purchase price must be able to pay off their loan. You need to know the actual loan payoff including any penalties and fees they may have incurred.

If your offer is not high enough, then you do not have a deal. Refer them to your Realtor friend and move on.

Moving

If the seller is relocating to a new area, perhaps because of a job transfer, then they may need to move quickly. In this case, you should focus on closing the deal as quickly as possible. You also must know what they *need* to walk away with. You could handle the conversation like this:

"Mr. Seller, my partner and I are very interested in your home. He has asked me to see if we can negotiate a mutually beneficial deal here.

By the way, when do you plan to move? Okay, I will make sure that we close on the property before that deadline.

What price do you absolutely need to get for the home? I will try my best to convince my partner to offer more if lines up with his investment criteria. I want to get you the best price possible."

Exhaustion or Frustration

Being a long-term landlord can become a burden over time. Some rental owners are sick and tired of dealing with tenants. They want out.

Here you come with a quick, cut-and-dried offer that releases them from this burden and gives them the cash to pursue hobbies that they will enjoy.

Find out if they have a bank loan and if so what the balance is on it. This will help you present an offer that will enable them to walk away without any reservations.

Depending on the owner's situation, you will need to present your offer in a different manner. Either way, remember that you are there to help the owner out of a stressful situation. Downplay the price and play up the benefits.

Writing the offer

This is the easy part, so stop and take a deep breath. You should have already prepared your Maximum Purchase Price. Decide if you want to start at that price or offer less. I advise to offer less counting on the fact that they will counter at a higher price. It is always easy to go up. Once the offer is accepted, however, you cannot go back down.

What Contract Should I Use?
You want your purchase contract to be legally binding. You also need it to look professional. You have three options:

Hire a Real Estate Attorney
A real estate attorney can draft your first purchase agreement. Then you can use this for all your future purchase offers. There will be an expense for this option.

Write your own.
You can prepare your own offer. I have seen some wholesalers prepare a simple one page form that states the buyer and seller's name and address, the property address and legal description, the purchase price and any contingencies and a closing date.

The problem here is that there are plenty of legal loopholes. Sellers may be leery of signing such an offer wondering if it is valid.

There are some online sites that have blank forms that may work, but you will need to check and make sure that all parts of the contract are legally binding in your state. A few websites that I recommend are:

> http://www.rocketlawyer.com/
> http://www.legalzoom.com/
> http://www.lawdepot.com

Get a Copy of the Contract Used by Realtors
This is the option that I recommend. Not only are you using the best legal purchase agreement in your state, but the seller, the title company and anyone else who will review the contract will be familiar with the format.

You may be able to get a copy of a contract from your Realtor friend. There may be a catch, however. Unless you submit an offer through them, it is doubtful that they will just give you one of their "private" forms. He or she will quickly assume that you are doing deals behind their back. So, find a doable property in the MLS and submit an offer. If it is rejected - oh well, too bad - but you will have a copy of the purchase agreement.

Before you can use this contract, however, make sure you remove all references to any board of realtors, MLS name or reference to any licensing board. Carefully read through the form to make sure that no where does it state that this offer has been prepared and submitted by a licensed real estate agent.

If you want, you could type this form into MS Word. Include all the legal mumbo-jumbo – which is the reason you are using this form in the first place.

Should I make offers under my name or set up a LLC?
Because of a fear of lawsuits, many buyers opt to purchase properties through a LLC. They think that if something goes sour, the courts will only have access to properties in the LLC. This thinking, however, is incorrect. The courts have recently been piercing through LLCs when they are owned and/or managed by only one individual. Because that person answers to only himself, they view the LLC as an extension of the person and thus it offers no protection.

Additionally, since you are never buying property – that is having title placed into your name – then there will never be property in your LLC. Having a LLC as a wholesaler is only an added complication. You can simply write all your offers using your own name.

There is one valid reason, however, for setting up an LLC as a wholesaler. If you are making offers on REO or bank owned properties, they will not allow you to assign the contract to another individual. One way around this is to form a LLC and then make your end buyer a member of the LLC. At closing, you "sell" or back out of the LLC for the value of your profit on the deal. Your end buyer's name is not on the title to the property, instead it is in the name of yours (now his) LLC.

Not only does this create an added transactional expense for you; but it can be difficult for the end buyer to get a loan. Also, if your end buyer plans to live in the property, they will not be eligible for a homestead exemption.

Only use a LLC as a wholesaler *if* you are buying a REO property *and* your end buyer will be setting up a LLC anyway.

If you locate an investment buyer before finding a seller, then discuss the option of submitting the offer under the LLC he plans to put his property in. You will also include a contingency that reads "Offer is subject to written approval of business partner within 7 days." Then, if your end buyer does not approve the purchase, the contract is void upon submitting it in writing to the seller. When the offer is given to the title company to arrange the closing, you would also submit an invoice for your fee (representing the profit for this deal).

What Types of Contingencies Should I Put in the Offer?

Because you are the middleman and not the end buyer, you need to write your offers in such a way that you have an exit strategy in the event that you cannot find an end buyer. You do not want to end up at closing and actually be liable for the $75,000 property you put an offer on.

Contingencies (or weasel clauses) will also give you the legal right to get back any earnest money that you put down to secure the property. If you just walk away from a deal without using a contingency, the seller will keep your earnest money.

The following contingencies will help to protect you:

... And/Or Assignees

This is a standard wholesaling marker for purchase agreements. These few words go right after your name under the "Buyer" line. This gives you the right to assign the contract to another person. This works great for FSBO properties but is a huge red light if you are submitting an offer through a licensed real estate agent. Also, REO properties do not allow this contingency.

Subject to a Satisfactory Inspection

"This offer is subject to a satisfactory inspection within 14 days after acceptance."

This is a standard contingency clause that every seller expects to see. You are not the one inspecting the property, your end buyer is the inspector. If they find something wrong with the property or you find something wrong with the property but cannot find an end buyer in time, you can use this contingency.

Note that this will need to be something valid, not "I don't like the stain on the counter" but rather items like cracks in the foundation, evidence of termites, faulty wiring, sagging floors etc. Also, put it in writing. This would either in the event that you waive the contingency or for the cancellation of the offer due to using the contingency.

Subject to Partner Approval

"Buyer's obligation to close this transaction is contingent upon contract approval by Buyer's partner. Buyer shall have 20 days after acceptance to approve or waive this contingency."

This contingency will give you some time to contact your end buyer and get them to commit to purchasing this property. I personally like this contingency because it puts the burden of closure on your end buyer.

Be aware that this contingency will not be accepted by all sellers, especially bank owned properties. Once again, acceptance or waiver of this contingency needs to be submitted to the seller in writing.

Subject to Financing
"Offer is contingent upon Buyer obtaining financing."

This is a pretty acceptable clause and is understood by 99.9% of sellers. If you cannot get bank financing, then you can back out of the offer.

It works well with FSBO properties but is no longer acceptable if offers are submitted through a real estate agency. Today, all sellers must be preapproved for a loan and that pre-approval should be attached to any offers submitted by a real estate agent.

I would not recommend including all of these contingencies in any given offer. Sellers do not like to accept offers that have lots of contingencies. This will also set off a warning bell if you have just convinced him or her that you will quickly close this deal and then you try to sneak in a 20 day contingency.

The success of closing deals will have much to do with having genuine end buyers lined up *before* you start putting offers on properties. This will limit the need for too many "weasel" clauses. We will talk about that more in the next chapter.

Do I need an Earnest Money deposit?
Earnest money deposits are a way buyers show sellers that they are serious about purchasing their property. If the buyer reneges on the deal without a just cause (i.e. contingencies clauses), then the seller can legally keep the earnest money.

Earnest money deposits can make inexperienced wholesalers feel nervous. They do not want to tie up money knowing that they will lose it if they cannot find an end buyer. (By the way, try really hard not to walk away from contracts, especially ones made through real estate agents – it will really trash your reputation.)

Here are some options to handle the Earnest Money Deposit:

Under the Earnest Money Deposit Write $0
This places no legal restrictions on you the buyer. It also tells the seller that you are not serious, are not committed to this offer or that you do not have any money.

There are wholesalers that do this all the time and it works for them. Just be forewarned that if the seller gets two offers at the identical price and one has an EMD and the other does not, they *will* chose the one with the EMD.

Put up a $100 to $500 Earnest Money Deposit
If you find that your $0 EMD offers are not being accepted, try putting up some money. Remember that you have your contingency clauses to back you up in case you need to be released from the contract.

Whatever money you put at the earnest deposit is *not* paid to the seller until closing. It should be deposited with whatever title company you use to complete the closing.

When you assign the contract, you submit an invoice to the title company indicating the amount of earnest money you put down. This will them be reimbursed to you at closing.

"An earnest money deposit of $x,xxx will be made upon the waiver of all the contingencies."
This is a way of telling the seller that you are serious about closing the transaction but have some reservations about the property.

"An earnest money deposit of $x,xxx will be made within 5 days from seller's acceptance."
If you have a buyer lined up then this is a great clause to give you a few days to get your assignment contract signed and receive the EMD from your end buyer. Sellers also will easily agree to this term.

Once you find your end buyer and you get them under contract, you take their EMD that they paid to you and assign it to your contract and then deposit it with the title company.

"The earnest money deposit of $x,xxx will be made upon contract approval from Buyer's partner."
I personally like this one. Your "buyer's partner" is your end buyer. Once they approve it by signing your wholesaler's contract, then you take the earnest money they paid you and assign it to your purchase contract with the seller. If you do not get your "partner's" approval, then the seller does not get the EMD. I even make a photocopy of a post dated check in the amount of the EMD and include it with the offer. Remember to blacken out the account number for safety.

Submitting Your Offer to the Seller

Once you have written your offer, it is now time to get it to the seller. Some wholesalers call the seller back (or meet with them in person) to talk about a purchase price. I believe this opens the door to receiving a barrage of unfavorable comments about how much his house is worth and how much you have insulted him with such a low offer.

Instead, submit your offers via email or snail mail. When initially talking to your seller, ask him if you could please submit an offer through email.

Do not just attach the offer and done. Include a letter something like this:

> *"Dear Seller,*
>
> *I am glad that we had a some time to talk about your property. I am interested in it very much. Attached is my purchase offer. Please take a moment to review it.*
>
> *As per our discussion, I realize that you need to sell because... I have carefully analyzed other properties in the area, calculated the cost of any repairs and met with my partner. This is the price that meets our investment guidelines and I hope that it will be acceptable to you as well.*
>
> *If you agree, please sign where indicated and email it back to this address. We will attempt to close the sale as soon as possible. Thank you for your time and consideration.*
>
> *Sincerely,*
>
> *(your name)"*

Give them a day or two to think about your offer. Then call him or her back to check to make sure they received it and that it did not end up in their junk mail folder. You can then proceed with the transaction either through a counter offer or proceeding forward with a signed contract.

Making multiple offers

Do not be afraid of submitting offers on multiple properties at the same time. Remember that you are not actually the one buying these properties. Having more than one property under contract at any given time will give your end buyers a greater selection to choose from and will show them that you are serious about finding them a property.

That being said, you need to be reasonably sure that you *can* locate a buyer for each property that you get under contract. That means that you need to know what buyers are looking for and in what price range they are seeking.

This also means that before you put your first offer on a property, you need to have located some buyers. This brings us to the next chapter.

CHAPTER 6 FINDING YOUR FIRST BUYER

Getting a buyer under contract is essential to wholesaling –or real estate in general, for that matter. Without a buyer, you do not have a transaction. Without a transaction, you do not make any money.

That is why you need to spend as much time and effort finding buyers as you do getting properties under contract.

What Comes First, the Seller or the Buyer?

This question mimics the "What comes first, the chicken or the egg?" Without the chicken to lay the egg, how did you get the egg? Without the egg, how did you get the chicken?

It is kind of the same conundrum with wholesaling. If you do not have a buyer, then the property you have under contract will expire. But, without a property under contract, how will you find a buyer?

That is why you must develop both sides of your business at the same time. Do not get a slew of properties under contract and then hope to find viable buyers within 2 weeks. Get your buyers lined up. Find out what they want. Then work with your seller contacts to get those types of properties under contract.

Finding Your Buyer

Just as there are different ways to locate a seller, so there are different marketing avenues to locate a buyer. This is by no means an exhaustive list, but it will get your juices rolling.

Craigslist Posts

You can find buyers one of two ways through Craigslist.

First, post *daily* ads that advertise that you have properties to wholesale. These are **general ads** to pull in a wide variety of buyers. Your ads could say "Wholesale Deals 70% of ARV" or "Single Family Homes for Sale below Market Prices." Include the general area where they are found (such as zip code, town or neighborhood). Then include your phone number and your website address if you have one.

Second, post *daily***ads for specific properties**. This would be for properties that you already have under contract. *Do not include the property address.* You do not want buyers to go to the owner directly. You can include pertinent facts such as size, bedrooms, bath, condition, garage, amenities, school district or if it is a rental property. You can even state that the property is X% below market value. Make sure you include your contact information.

Property Management Companies

Make a list of all of the property management companies in your market area. Give them a call to see if any of their clients are interested in buying more investment properties. Let them know that you have some really good deals and you would like to give their client's an opportunity to snatch them up.

If they are reluctant to give out names and phone numbers, ask them if you could send them a list of what you have available and if their clients have interest, they could give you a call. Then put together a stunning marketing package. Remember, no property addresses. Even photographs of the exterior of the home can be a giveaway.

Landords

Buy and hold investors (also known as landlords) tend to keep acquiring properties, especially profitable ones. This can be an excellent source of buyers. You can locate landlords through property managers like we mentioned above or you can find them yourself.

Head on down to the county Register of Deeds or Tax Assessor's office to locate the area landlords. Do a records sort based on the owner's name. Now look for the same individual who owns multiple properties. (Make sure these are improved sites and not just vacant lots.) Write down their name and mail them a well written cover letter and the same marketing material that you sent to the property management companies.

Then, go online and do a reverse directory search off their address and see if you can locate their phone number. After mailing your package to them, wait a couple of days and then give them a call.

If they are not interested in any of your properties, ask them if they are looking for any specific types of properties. Tell them that you come across great deals all the time and you would be glad to keep your eyes open for something that he is looking for.

Another method of locating landlords is to call on rental ads. You can find them when you are driving around, when you read the classifieds in the paper or online. Remember, this is also a great way to find sellers as well.

Use Social Networking

Facebook and Twitter are not just for friends to stay in touch; it also is a great viral advertising tool. By creating pages and then posting the properties that you have under contract (no addresses, remember), you can have basically free advertising to your "friends" and your "friend's friends." LinkedIn is another excellent resource.

You can also search through these sites and join groups that look like great sources of leads – both sellers and buyers. Do not just focus on hawking your contracts, be a contributing member. Focus on education, mentoring and providing advice. Nothing builds a strong internet presence than that.

Join Your Local REIA
The National Real Estate Investors Organization is a non-profit Trade Association for real estate investors. Not only do they provide some really educational seminars, but it is a great place to network with investors and other real estate professionals.

Google Adwords
So far, all our advertising methods have been free. They may require some thought, time and effort but they do not cost you anything. Google Adwords, on the other hand, is not a free method of advertising, but it can be super effective.

Adwords is a very specific form of pay-per-click advertising. You can narrow your ad placements by almost any type of demographics including specific websites, keywords or even location (as in only surfers that live in specific areas will see your ad).

Google Adwords also has a great set of analytics. Each ad within a campaign is measured. You can readily tell if it is effective. You can even tweak your ads and see which call to action is the most effective. Guess what? You can then use that information in your mass mailings.

You have the option of having text ads which show up when a surfer does a Google search. To use this, you need to setup some specific keywords. Google can help you with this as well. You can also create display ads. You can design your own or pick from some pretty neat templates.

Bandit Signs
Bandit signs are not just to find sellers. You can use them to get buyers as well. Some buyers will call off your "We Buy Cheap Houses" signs. You can also create buyer specific signs that would be similar to your general Craigslist ads. Use the same color scheme as your seller bandit signs so that people link the two with the same company.

Networking is the Key
If you want to locate buyers, then you will need to network. Word of mouth is by far the best form of advertising. The only way people are going to talk about you is if you start talking to people.

Make friends, be friendly. Spread the word that you are looking for homes to buy and that you have contracts for below market homes that you are willing to sell. The more word you get out, the more word will spread.

Create a Buyer's List
Once you start tracking down some potential buyers, you need to keep track of them. Though you can use Post-It notes, I wouldn't recommend it. That buyer's note that dropped behind the desk could have been the one for your new contract.

Once again, having a good CRM software system will help considerably. You will be able to create criteria for your purchasers and then be able to search based on that criteria. It will also track how often they have been contacted. There is a fine line between staying visible and stalking. Don't cross the line.

You need to have a system setup to monitor and track your buyer, their address, phone number, email and property requirements. Then, keep in touch with your buyers. Even if they said they are not looking right now – just wait until you show them the perfect property – bet you they will change their mind.

Also, keep in touch with your buyers on a regular basis. This could be through monthly newsletters or well timed phone calls. But no matter what method you choose, make sure it is consistent and productive.

CHAPTER 7 YOUR WHOLESALE CONTRACT

So, you have your property under a purchase contract. You have found an end buyer who is willing to buy your contract. Now, the question is "How do you write the wholesale or end buyer's contract? How is it different from your purchase agreement?"

There are two ways you can get your end buyer under contract. The first is through an Assignment of Contract and the other is by preparing another Purchase Agreement for your end buyer.

What Contract to Use
Which option you choose will depend much on how you setup your original purchase agreement with the seller and how you intend to close the property.

Assignment of Contract
If your purchase agreement with the seller allows you to assign the contract, then this is by far the easiest way to complete your wholesale transaction.

- Traditional simple closing.
- You are paid via an invoice submitted to the title agency payable at the closing.
- You do not need to be at the closing, your check can be mailed to you.
- But, your end buyer will be able to see your purchase price.

End Buyer Purchase Agreement
If your purchase agreement with the seller did not allow for an assignment or your offer was made on a REO

property, then you will need to "resell" or flip the property to your end buyer by using another purchase agreement.

- Requires either a hard money loan to close with the seller or a double close (we will explain this a little later).
- Your payment is the difference between the first contract and your second purchase agreement, payable at closing.
- You must be present at closing.
- The end buyer does not know your purchase price.
- But, you must find a title company that is willing to process a double closing.

Using an Assignment of Contract

Using an Assignment of Contract eliminates the need to do a double close. A double close is when you first close the transaction with the seller and then immediately close a second transaction with your end buyer.

These types of transactions necessitate a cooperative title company (i.e. one who is willing to close the first transaction without funds knowing that the second transaction will pay for the first) or you personally will need a hard money loan to pay for the first deal.

Before you can assign a contract, you must have stated that intention in your purchase agreement with the seller. You can put it under the purchaser's name, as in "(You Name) and/or assigns" or as a statement in the addendum "Purchaser reserves the right to assign this contract." Without that term, you may not be able to assign it. So unless it is a REO or bank owned property, make sure that clause is in all of your purchase agreements.

Where to Get the Form

Just as Purchase Agreements are state specific, so are Assignment of Contract forms. You can do a search online for one approved to be used in your state or you can contact a real estate attorney and have him draft a copy for you. You can then use copy for other transactions.

Earnest Money Deposit

Whether or not you put down an earnest money deposit with the seller is immaterial. You do, however, want to make sure that your end buyer puts down an earnest money deposit. You do not want them to back out leaving you stuck holding a legal agreement to purchase real estate that you had no intention of owning.

Many wholesalers state in their contract that the EMD is non-refundable unless seller cannot provide clear title.

The earnest money deposit is paid by your end buyer to the title company that you will be using at closing. It will be applied to the purchase price on the closing statements.

Assignment Fee

In the addendum section of the assignment contract with your end buyer, you need to state that "At closing, (Your Name) will receive an assignment fee of $x,xxx." The assignment fee is the difference between your original purchase price and your end buyer's purchase price. It is important to include the assignment fee in your contract.

The more you are making on this deal, the less your end buyer may like your assignment fee. If you stand to make over $5,000 on this transaction, I would recommend using a separate purchase agreement and doing a double closing.

When you submit the Assignment of Contact document to the title company, include an invoice for your Assignment Fee.

When an Assignment Fee is Not Allowed

It is important to mention that if your end buyer is getting financing for his or her purchase, their lender may not allow the payment of an assignment fee. In this case, include your assignment fee as part of their earnest money deposit.

For example,

> You paid a $100 earnest money deposit to the seller.

> The difference between your purchase price and your end buyer's purchase price is $5,000.

> Your end buyer's non-refundable EMD would be $5,100.

> You would submit an invoice to the title company for $5,100 and get paid at closing.

Note, do not label this as a "finder's fee." This is too close to the duties of a licensed real estate agent. You do not want to be accused of selling real estate. It is an assignment fee.

Notify the Seller

Once you have your end buyer's signature on the Assignment of Contract document, you will need to provide written notification to the seller to let him know that you are not longer completing the transaction but have assigned it to another buyer. Many wholesalers include this acknowledgement right on the Assignment of Contract form. They have a place for all three parties to sign (the seller, you and your end buyer).

Using an Additional Purchase Agreement

You will need to pursue this route IF the seller will not allow an assignment of contract (i.e. bank owned properties), an assignment clause was not part of your purchase agreement (oops) or your profit is too high and would freak out the end buyer (you contracted for $15,000 and assigned it for $35,000 and are showing an assignment fee of $20,000).

If you are faced with any of those situations, then you will need to complete a double close and create a new purchase agreement.

Where to Get the Form

You can use the same blank form as you did when you created your purchase contract with the seller.

Earnest Money Deposit

At a minimum, you need your end buyer to pay at least the same amount that you paid to the seller. Ideally, you would like to have your end buyer pay more. That way, if they back out at the last minute, you will not have to pay for any title company fees for cancelling the closing nor will you "lose" your earnest money deposit.

Some wholesalers make sure that their end buyers are committed to completing the transaction by making their earnest money deposit non-refundable unless seller cannot guarantee clear title.

Contingencies

Because you are initiating a new transaction with your end buyer, you are still responsible for your contingencies with the seller. That being said, you do not want your end buyer's contingencies to extend beyond yours.

For example, if you have a 14 day inspection period and your end buyer signs his contract 4 days later, his inspection contingency cannot be any longer than 10 days.

Do not allow your end buyer to include a finance contingency unless they have a pre-approval letter from their lender.

The fewer contingencies you get from your end buyer, the better for you. Your objective here is to make sure your end buyer is committed to completing the transaction. You do not want them to put in any "weasel" clauses to get out.

How You Get Paid

On an Assignment of Contract, you are paid an assignment fee at closing. Things are a little different when you initiate a separate purchase agreement with your end buyer.

You will still get paid at closing, but it is not a fee rather it is the profit from the two transactions.

For example, if you purchase a home from the seller for $15,000 and resell it for $35,000, then the difference from these two transactions will be $20,000 less any closing costs that you are responsible for. That is the cash in your hand when you leave the title company.

CHAPTER 8 CLOSING THE DEAL

You are not in the home stretch. You can see the finish line. You can smell the sweet scent of victory. All you have to do now is close the deal and take home your money.

Traditional Closings vs. the Double Close

There are two basic ways a wholesaler will close a deal. The easiest method is via a traditional closing. The other is perhaps a little more complicated but just as effective. It is called the double close.

Traditional Closings

This closing is just like any other traditional property purchase. The signed purchase agreement, the Assignment of Contract and your invoice for the assignment fee are all delivered to the title company. They check for transferable title and prepare the closing documents in the end buyer's name.

The seller and your end buyer meet at the title company on the scheduled closing date. They sign all the documents. You do not need to be there. The title company will mail you a check.

Double Closings

This closing is a non-traditional closing and not every title company will handle double closings. You not only need to understand how one works, but you will also need to find a title company in your area that is willing to complete a double closing. This emphasizes the point that it is important that *you* choose the title company, not the seller.

A double close is just what it sounds like. It is two closings at almost the exact same moment and that are financially linked. This type of closing is used any time you are not able to assign a contract.

The initial steps are just like with a traditional closing. The title company receives a copy of each purchase agreement. They prepare closing documents between you and the seller *and* between you and your end buyer.

The title company will then schedule both closings to happen on the same day and back to back.

First, you will close the transaction with the seller. The title company will present the seller with a check in the amount of your purchase price less any closing costs.

Then, as the seller walks out of the room, in comes your end buyer. He then signs all of the documents for his purchase. He presents the title company with a check that covers your purchase price that was already paid to the seller and your profit margin – less any closing costs that you have incurred. The title company will give you a check for that amount.

As you can see, in this scenario, you do not have to bring any money to the closing. The title company "floats" the first transaction. There is a considerable amount of risk here for the title company, so do not be surprised if they will want to make sure that your end buyer is sitting in the office and that he or she has all the necessary funds right then and there.

Instances When You Will Need a Hard Money Loan
There are some transactions that may require you to obtain a hard money loan.

- ⬜ The title company will not do a double close.
- ⬜ The end buyer cannot close the transaction on the same day as you and the seller close.
- ⬜ You could not locate a buyer but do not want to lose the deal.

To handle transactions like these, you will need to actually *pay* for the property and then resell the property to your end buyer to get your money out of it plus your profit margin.

You could get traditional bank financing. You will need to meet all of the lender's loan requirements including down payment, credit rating and debt to income ratios. You must also make sure that there are not pre-payment penalties.

If that seems like a pain, and often it is for a wholesaler, then perhaps you should consider a hard money loan. Hard money lenders are less concerned with your credit rating and more concerned with a rapid payoff and a large return. That makes obtaining a hard money loan often easier than traditional bank funding.

On the flip side of the coin, however, is the fact that hard money loans can be quite expense. Not only are the closing costs high but the interest rate will much higher than conventional loan rates.

Hard money loans are a great option if you need quick funding to pull off a deal. They are not a very good option for length transactions, fix and flips or buy and holds.

Title Insurance

Depending on the state where you live, you may or may not be required to get title insurance. In my opinion, it is well worth the expense – for your end buyer that is.

Title insurance is a two-fold policy. First, the title company will run a title check on the parcel. This will bring up any problems in the chain of title or if there are any liens against the property. Title insurance can only be placed on a property that can be transferred free of liens and clouds on the title.

Secondly, title insurance protects the owner against anything that the title company may have missed. For example, if Uncle Edward never signed off on the title back when it sold in 1952, your title insurance policy will handle and pay for whatever it takes to clear the title.

The thing with wholesaling is that you as the middleman do not need title insurance. But, you should recommend that your end buyer invest in the policy. It is a one-time fee at closing and the policy continues until ownership changes on the property.

Now, if you suspect that the owner of the property has not been upfront with any past liens *and* the law does not require such *and* you end buyer refuses to pay for a title insurance policy, I would recommend investing in a title search. This will cost around $100 and it will show you any liens that are on the property and who are on the title. You should be able to get your end buyer to pay for that. The title company will just put it on his closing statement.

Getting Paid

"Getting paid." Sounds good doesn't it? After all that hard work, time and effort, that first check will be so sweet.

As we have discussed, unless you can convince your end buyer to pay you upfront when you transfer the contract, you will get your check at closing. Spend it well.

Getting Started

So, that's the essential steps to wholesaling. Once you understand the concepts, it is just a matter of creating the systems to keep farming for buyers and sellers and getting them under contracts.

Like any potential business venture, it is easy to sit on the sofa and dream about the business and the success. But that is all it will be is dreams unless you get up and get working.

Wholesaling is a realistic business opportunity. It works and there are plenty of people out there that prove that it works. It is not easy money. It is not a get rich quick scheme. It is, however, great way to get into real estate with very little money upfront. It is an excellent way to build experience, skills and cash to move into even larger real estate investments.

In talking to other wholesalers and mentors, it seems that the advice I hear over and over is this.

You do not need to know everything to start.
That is so true. What you have learned in this guide is all you need to learn to get started. It is the basic steps to success. Yes, you will learn as you go. You will make mistakes, say the wrong things, contract the bad deals – but you will be wholesaling and every deal closed will build confidence and skill. So take what you know now and start!

Develop and Stick to Systems.
This is an easy piece advice to overlook but it is a critical one nonetheless. In order to stay on top of all your client leads, marketing projects and buyer contracts, you need an efficient system. Find a way to manage each piece of the puzzle. Make sure that not one contact is lost or forgotten. Write down the steps to each system and then follow it religiously. It is time well spent and will greatly increase your profitability.

**You are in the Marketing Business...
not the Real Estate Business.**

Does that sound familiar? It should. We have tried to impress that upon you from the beginning. Realtors sell real estate and they need a license to do it.

You are not a licensed real estate agent and you don't have to be. You are in the business of selling contracts, real estate contracts to be specific. You are selling your contracted interest in a piece of real estate.

Keep that in mind when you write up your marketing pieces. Keep it in mind when you talk to your buyers and sellers. Do not lead them to think that you are their Realtor.

Also, because you are in the marketing business – that should be your prime focus. Marketing is the life blood of wholesaling. If you do not continuously market for buyers and sellers, you business will stall and you will get hungry and homeless. Focus on marketing and the rest of the parts will fall in place.

You now know what you need to know to start wholesaling. I wish you the best of luck and the greatest of success.

Now get out there and find a seller!

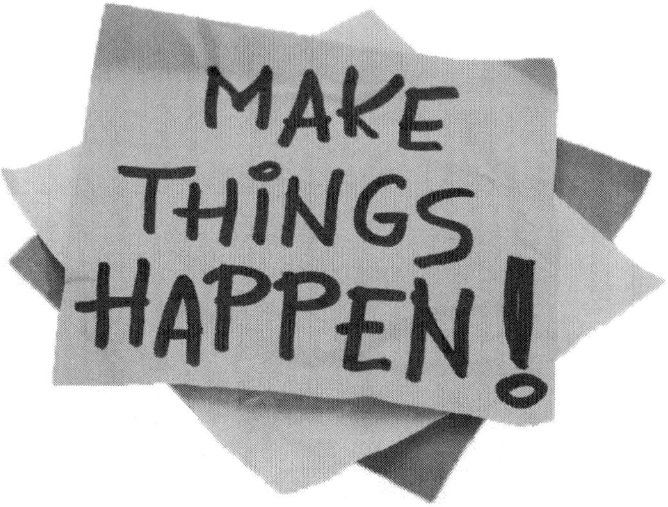
MAKE THINGS HAPPEN!

Made in the USA
San Bernardino, CA
15 April 2017